DOGS SET IV

Greyhounds

Cari Meister
ABDO Publishing Company

visit us at
www.abdopub.com

Published by ABDO Publishing Company, 4940 Viking Drive, Suite 622, Edina, Minnesota 55435. Copyright © 2001 Abdo Consulting Group, Inc. International copyrights reserved in all countries. No part of this book may be reproduced in any form without written permission from the publisher.

Printed in the United States.

Cover Photo: Animals Animals©Robert Maier
Interior Photos: Animals Animals©Fritz Prenzel (page 5), Animals Animals©Robert Pearcy (page 11), Animals Animals©Carol Geake (page 15), Animals Animals©Robert Pearcy (page 21); Corbis (pages 9, 13, 17); AP/Wideworld (pages 7, 19)

Editors: Tamara L. Britton, Kate A. Furlong, Christine Fournier
Art Direction: Neil Klinepier

Library of Congress Cataloging-in-Publication Data

Meister, Cari.
   Greyhounds / Cari Meister.
      p. cm. -- (Dogs, Set IV)
   Includes bibliographical references and index.
   ISBN 1-57765-473-0
    1. Greyhounds--Juvenile literature. [1. Greyhounds. 2. Dogs.] I. Title.

SF429.G8 M45 2001
636.753'4--dc21

                                                                00-045381

Contents

The Dog Family

Thousands of years ago, people tamed wild dogs. They trained their dogs to help them do work, such as herding and hunting. People also tamed dogs to be their companions and friends. Today, more than 400 different dog breeds exist.

All dogs belong to the **family** called Canidae. Members of this family are called canids. Wolves, foxes, dingoes, and jackals are also canids. Canids share some of the same **traits**.

Canids are pack animals. That means they like to be part of a group. For pet dogs, their pack is their human family. Even though greyhounds are bred for dog shows or racing, they can also be a fun part of your family.

Greyhounds have many of the same traits as other canids.

Greyhounds

Greyhounds are one of the oldest dog breeds. In Egypt, **tomb** carvings show greyhounds hunting deer. Some of the carvings are more than 4,000 years old! In time, greyhounds spread to other parts of Africa, Europe, and the Middle East.

People bred greyhounds to run fast. They used greyhounds to hunt for food. Greyhounds hunted using their keen sense of sight rather than their sense of smell. They could easily catch deer, rabbits, and other small animals.

In ancient Europe, greyhounds were used in a sport called coursing. In coursing, greyhounds are placed on a set course. They hunt for small game, such as rabbits.

Today, some owners exhibit their greyhounds at dog shows. Other owners race their greyhounds on courses and tracks. Today's greyhound racers usually chase **lures** instead of live game. People often adopt retired racers as pets.

Greyhounds racing on a track

What They're Like

Greyhounds are swift, graceful, intelligent dogs. Most greyhounds are bred to be racing dogs. Some are bred to be show dogs. But few are bred to be family pets.

Greyhounds are quiet dogs that like to rest. They usually bark only when something is wrong. They spend most of the day lying around sleeping.

Many greyhounds are **sensitive**. They get scared easily. Greyhounds do not **respond** well to loud noises or rough handling. Greyhounds need lots of encouragement and praise.

Greyhounds get along well with quiet, older children. They rarely fight with other dogs. And greyhounds can be trained to get along with cats.

Greyhounds are bred to race, but they make great pets, too!

Coat and Color

Greyhounds have a short, fine coat. It does not shed often. But it does tear and rip easily. So greyhounds must be **groomed** very gently.

A greyhound's coat is not oily. Little dirt or oil can cling to it. This means that greyhounds rarely have a doggy smell.

Greyhounds are not just gray. They come in many colors! Greyhounds can be any color from white to black. They can also be red, **fawn**, or brown.

Greyhounds can have many different patterns on their coats. Some greyhounds are **brindle**. Some are one solid color. Other greyhounds have patches of different colors.

A greyhound with a brindle coat

Size

A greyhound is tall, sleek, and **muscular**. It has a narrow head and long neck. Its small ears stand straight up. It has a long tail. It has small, rounded feet and long legs. Its arched back is very limber.

Male greyhounds stand between 27 and 30 inches (69-76 cm) tall. They weigh between 65 and 70 pounds (30-32 kg). Female greyhounds stand between 26 and 28 inches (66-71 cm) tall. They weigh 55 to 65 pounds (25-30 kg).

Greyhounds can run up to 45 miles per hour (117 km/h)! They are so fast because they have more muscle and less fat than most other breeds.

Greyhounds are also fast because their limber backs and long legs allow them to run at a **double**

suspension gallop. This kind of running is very tiring. So greyhounds are better **sprinters** than long-distance runners.

The greyhound's build makes it the fastest dog in the world.

Care

Most greyhounds are **sensitive**. A person caring for and training a greyhound must always remember its sensitive nature. A firm "no" is often the only **discipline** a greyhound needs.

Keeping up a **routine** is important in caring for a greyhound. At the racetrack, greyhounds have set times for exercise and feeding. Retired greyhounds that are adopted as pets should have a routine at their new home, too.

A greyhound's short coat needs little brushing. Usually brushing a greyhound once a week is enough. But make sure to use only a soft brush or glove to avoid hurting the greyhound's thin skin.

Like all dogs, greyhounds need to visit the **veterinarian** every year. The veterinarian will check to make sure the dog is healthy.

Greyhounds need plenty of time to run and play.

Feeding

Greyhounds should eat a dog food made of meat. Dry food is best for their teeth. But retired racers may be used to real meat and may dislike dry dog food. Mixing dry dog food and canned dog food for awhile may help.

Greyhounds should be fed twice a day. Because they are so tall, it is a good idea to place their food on a block of wood 6 inches (15 cm) off the ground. That way, they do not have to bend down so far to eat. Always have fresh water near their food.

Greyhounds are naturally trim dogs. It is important not to overfeed greyhounds. They **respond** poorly to being overweight.

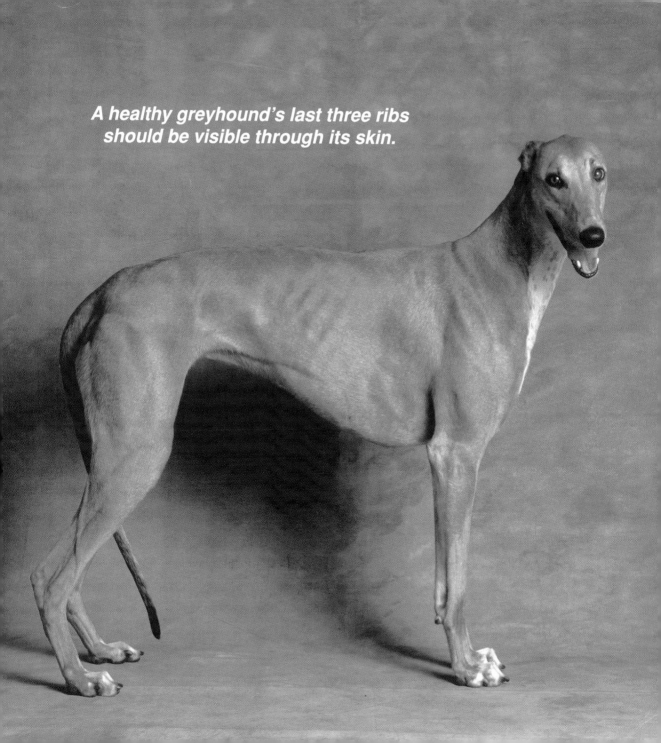

A healthy greyhound's last three ribs should be visible through its skin.

Things They Need

Often greyhounds are called the world's fastest couch potato. Greyhounds love to lay around and sleep. But they need exercise, too.

Greyhounds can run away easily. They will chase a small animal, such as a squirrel, for miles. So a greyhound must always be walked on a leash. And it must only run in a fenced area.

Greyhounds need large, soft, padded beds. They do not have much fat on their bodies. So greyhounds can get bedsores if they do not have a soft place to rest.

With so little body fat, greyhounds do not have much **insulation**. They get hot and cold easily. So it's best if they live inside. In cold weather, a greyhound should wear a coat to keep warm.

A greyhound spends most of the day resting and saving its energy. This allows it to run at fast speeds later.

Puppies

Most greyhound puppies are raised to show or race. So they have a very different early life than many other dogs.

After a racing greyhound is **weaned**, it prepares to race. Most early training sessions involve play. Some trainers give greyhound puppies stuffed toys to chase. Other trainers attach a stuffed toy to a string. Puppies bat at the toy and run after it.

When racing puppies are about four months old, they learn to walk on a leash. They play with other puppies to get strong. Between 10 and 12 months of age, the puppies start their real training. Their life becomes a **routine** of running, playing, eating, and sleeping.

Greyhound puppies

Glossary

brindle: a gray, tan, or tawny color with darker streaks or spots.

discipline: to train or exercise in order to gain obedience.

double suspension gallop: a type of running where the greyhound's feet leave the ground twice in one gallop. Most breeds' feet leave the ground only once.

family: a group that scientists use to classify similar plants and animals. It ranks above a genus and below an order.

fawn: a light, yellowish-brown color.

groom: to clean and condition.

insulation: a material that keeps something from losing heat.

lure: a bait used to lead an animal in a certain direction.

muscular: having many well-defined muscles.

respond: to act in answer.

routine: a fixed method of doing things.

sensitive: easily hurt or offended.

sprinter: a person or animal that can run at top speed for a short distance.

tomb: a large chamber where a person is buried.

trait: a feature of an animal.

wean: to accustom an animal to eating food other than its mother's milk.

veterinarian: a doctor who takes care of animals.

Internet Sites

Greyhound Adoption Center
http://www.greyhoundog.org
This is the site of one of the largest and oldest greyhound rescue groups in the U.S. Find out all about retired racing greyhounds and what kind of care they need.

A Breed Apart
http://www.abap.org/framestart.htm
This is an online magazine for greyhound owners. Read interesting greyhound trivia, or articles about training and caring for greyhounds.

Online Dog-owner's Guide
http://www.canismajor.com/dog/ghound.html
Learn about greyhounds' personality, care, racing, and more. This site also has a list of further reading about greyhounds.

These sites are subject to change. Go to your favorite search engine and type in greyhounds for more sites.

Index